KINGDOM PRINCIPLES FROM

THE DRIVER'S SEAT

GOING ON AN ADVENTURE WITH GOD

ABIGAEL AKINTOLA

Published by Brandives
www.brandives.com or email: brandives.agency@gmail.com
Ontario, Canada

To contact the Author, Abigael Akintola.
Email: abigael.akintola23@gmail.com
Facebook: https://www.facebook.com/abigael.oludeyi23
Instagram: @abigael.akintola23
Website: www.mastersfeetnetwork.org

ISBN 978-1-7387546-3-2

Contents

Foreword

The opening line of a song often sang by our Songster Brigade, which is what we in The Salvation Army call our choirs, is: "Life is a journey, long is the road..." Upon singing those words, my mind was often drawn back to the days when my family would head for a road trip, which in Northern Ireland was not a considerable distance. However, for us, any trip was an occasion for song, because our car – as most in those days – did not have a radio. Yes, at one time cars were only for getting from point 'A' to point 'B', not made to be mobile entertainment centers. Those hours spent singing and conversing were formational for our lives, for the songs we sang were Sunday School songs and the stories exchanged usually were seasoned with Bible lessons. Whether on purpose or not, my parents practiced the advice of Moses:

"These commandments that I give you today are to be upon your hearts. Impress them on your children. Talk about them when you sit [in traffic] and when you [drive] along the road, when you [slow] down and when you [speed] up." (Deuteronomy 6:6-7, The Vauxhall Paraphrase).

Life, like the road, is filled with many routes, detours, bumps, construction zones, and fellow travelers we meet on the journey. One leg of my journey led me through Saskatoon, where for four years it was my privilege to meet a wonderful family from Nigeria, who were on their own journey. For four years, they faithfully attended Saskatoon Temple, and we were able to both witness and share in more than a few mile markers of their lives, such as visits from family 'back home', graduations, marriages, and the arrival of additional passengers i.e. children. As their pastors, it was the privilege of my wife and me to participate in the blessing of the first of those children, in a wonderful ceremony that clearly demonstrated the central role that faith played in their lives.

As the various names were being read by their father from around the globe in Nigeria (via the wonder of modern communication), we noticed a repetitive prefix, that upon query, I learned was the Nigerian term for 'God.' Therefore, many of the names each reflected a particular blessing or prayer to God for and upon the child. It almost made me wish I had been born in Benin rather than Belfast (though, to be truthful, those deliciously roasted sweet potatoes that turned out to be plantains were enough to woo me).

Over the years we watched a shy young university student blossom into a beautiful bride, a godly mother, conference organizer, and now an author. I had the honor of being asked by her to speak at the initial "Light Up Conference", and I am, once again, honored to add my humble thoughts to this latest offering.

As in her previous book Life Lessons from Biblical Encounters, Abigael draws from the rich store of treasures from the Bible, and the characters found therein, weaving them together with practical experiences of daily life in our time, and informed from her own life experience. With this latest offering, she illustrates spiritual truths using a practice to which all can relate – driving a car.

As Abigael points out, Jesus, the master illustrator, and storyteller would often put hooks into the mundane of life so as to transform them into powerful lessons. Kyle Snodgrass notes that the parables of Jesus "are handles for understanding his teaching on the kingdom." (Snodgrass, Klyne R.. Stories with Intent . Wm. B. Eerdmans Publishing Co.. Kindle Edition.) Abigael has successfully molded parables and illustrations into car door handles. Thus, checking our blind spot has taken on even greater meaning and importance, as has the rear-view mirror, warning lights, road signs, stopping for gas, and much more.

All of us are on a journey somewhere. You will find here new and enlightening ways to reflect upon that journey and the importance of faith on the way. I recommend this book as a way to inform your conversation (if you dare turn off the ubiquitous entertainment system) and possibly enrich the journey for driver and passenger, as you travel along the road. And while you may not be any more pleased to pay your annual insurance bill, at least now the sting may be somewhat soothed by the reminder of the assurance we have in salvation, provided at no cost to us, by our Lord, Redeemer, and Saviour, Jesus Christ. Enjoy the journey, and pray we can sing the songs of Zion together when we reach our destination.

Major Gerald Reilly,
Corps Officer
The Salvation Army
Mississippi-Rideau Lake Corps
Smiths Falls, ON

Dedication

This book is dedicated to God the Father, God the Son, and God the Holy Spirit – the sole source of my inspiration – whose desire is to share the core of their hearts with the world.

Introduction

God uses storylines and life's experiences to illustrate principles of the Kingdom and because stories resonate with humans, they bring knowledge using what we can relate with. Have you ever wondered why Jesus used proverbs to describe the principles and concepts of the Kingdom? I believe it's because stories are relatable and teach us complex concepts in simple ways. I have found that most people forget complex subjects, songs, quotes, and messages but it's always easy for them to remember simple stories because they can easily relate to some objects or identities mentioned in the story. Many times when I am on the road while driving or in a car, God shares some vital life lessons and Kingdom principles with me, illustrating them using rules and regulations on driving on the road, perhaps because life itself is a journey.

This book is a chronicle of some of what I have been taught while at the driver's seat. The book was written according to the inspiration of the Holy Spirit and the revelation of God's Word. Each chapter of the book defines and illustrates some important concepts in the Christian journey with short stories that we can relate to. These topics include faith, wisdom, spiritual sensitiveness, safety, obedience to, and reflection on God's Word. The lives of the three patriarchs of faith, Abraham, Isaac, and Jacob are great examples that demand reflection. These three generations of men walked with God and followed God's principles. These principles do not only build us for our spiritual journey but also shape our lives as a whole. God is a God of dimensions who is not only interested in our spiritual life but takes up our life as His project when we surrender ourselves to Him.

As you journey through this book, I trust God to open the eyes of your understanding and enlighten you more in order to come to the knowledge and revelation of His Word beyond the stories, illustrations, and letters inscribed on each page. The Holy Spirit, who is the main author of this book, will inspire you and guide you through your life's journey to bring you to safety.

CHAPTER 1

Zoom In

On a cold fall afternoon in 2012, I had earlier contacted a phone seller to pick up a phone at his residence. So, I went with three of my siblings and a friend. My elder sister was driving, and I was right behind her. We were about 5 minutes away from the seller's residence and we needed to turn left at the traffic light. My sister had to wait a while because of oncoming cars on the other lane of the road. There was a car coming behind us and the next thing we heard was the sound of a collision. I and a few of my siblings went black out for a few seconds. I opened my eyes and I asked, "What just happened?" We got out of the car and we noticed that our car had been hit with a high impact. The back of our car was a complete write-off. I looked at the car that hit us, it was a brand new car and the driver had two of his kids in the car. Looking at his car, I noticed the airbag of the car had popped out of the steering wheel and his gas was leaking. We had to move back from the leaking gas in case an explosion occurred. The owner of the car was confused and he said, "I'm sorry guys, I saw you driving right in front of me but one of my kids told me to look at something by the road side and I got distracted." He acknowledged that it was his fault and he felt guilty that he took his eyes off the road to get distracted by something else. An action that cost him dearly. He kept asking, "Are you guys alright?" At that instant, I knew it could have happened to anyone. Most times when we drive, we sometimes take our eyes off the windshield to either check the rear-view mirror or the side mirrors to see what is happening around us. While waiting for the cops to come, I was wondering about what happened in that little time. When the cops came, he asked us what happened and he went to the man to ask for his side of the story. He told him exactly what he had told us. The cops asked if we needed to see a doctor, but we said we were fine (so I thought). The cops requested our details and he said we should report to our insurance company. Although I was not feeling too good, I had to drive everyone home because my sister was still in shock. A few days later, I had to make a presentation to a group of people and I just went blank. My supervisor asked me what happened, and I told her I was involved in an accident a few days back. She requested that I see a doctor immediately after which I was medically fit to return to school and work. I could easily relate to this quote that states that remember that the windshield is bigger than the rear-view mirror because where you are going is more important than where you are coming from. Many people lose their vision because they lose focus on the one who gave them the vision. Most of the incidents in our lives have Biblical references, the story of Peter walking on the sea resonates very well with this story of my life and the quote.

According to Matthew's account of the story of how Jesus and Peter walked on the sea, in Matthew 14: 22 – 26, Jesus went to the mountain to pray while he sent his disciples to go ahead of him to Capernaum. The wind was against their boat before Jesus went to meet them (v. 24). Amid the storm, they were terrified to see Jesus walking on the sea and they cried out in fear, It's a ghost. Jesus revealed his identity to them, and He told them not to be afraid. Peter then replied, Lord if it's you, tell me to come to you on water. Oftentimes, we find ourselves seeking to know if the voice we perceive in our spirit is God's or not - The "God, if this is truly you, show me signs" or "Testing the spirits" syndrome. Peter wanted to be sure it was truly Jesus.

Jesus said, "Come!" In most of life's situations, God always gives us a word to hold onto. In this case, Jesus didn't say, Peter, you should know it's me, why are you doubting me? Can't you remember some of my past miracles? No, Jesus only said, Come. In most cases, we expect God to give us words that we are expecting but His response might just be "Peace" while we are waiting for fully detailed sentences. What word has the Lord spoken to you concerning your life's situation? It might be simple, but act it out in faith to experience the supernatural.

Romans 10: 17
So then faith comes by hearing, and hearing by the word of God.

At that point, when Jesus bid him come, Peter stepped out of the boat in faith to meet the Lord. He was leaving the known for the unknown. However, being a fisherman who had experience about the sea and how impossible it is for anyone to walk on water, Peter couldn't wrap his head around that action. While Peter was walking on water, he got distracted by the wind and he started sinking. At this point, Peter zoomed in on fear and zoomed out on faith. Faith and fear cannot live in the same heart. It's like light and darkness, when the light comes in, darkness fades away. How often do we try to wrap our heads around what God has made possible by calling it impossible due to our experience or knowledge or expertise? God can defy any law or common sense. Has the law of gravity been able to explain Jesus' walking on the sea or medical expertise to define how Lazarus came back to life after 4 days? Chemistry has not been able to explain the process behind water being turned to wine. The law of Economics and Finances can never explain how Peter was able to pay the temple tax from the money he picked from the mouth of the fish according to Jesus' instruction.

In a world where we are being tossed by waves and turbulence, we can't afford to take our eyes off Jesus who is our anchor in the midst of a storm. That is the time we need to focus on the one whom the winds and the waves obey. Matthew 8:27

It's easier to trust God when there is food on our tables, we are debt-free and things are working for us. What happens when unforeseen life situations press in; unpaid bills, bad medical reports, unemployment, academic failure, immigration issues, and pressures? How strong and concentrating is our faith when we walk through the valley of the shadow of death or when we are at quarter to shame?

Hebrews 12: 2

Looking unto Jesus the author and finisher of our faith; who for the joy that was set before him endured the cross, despising the shame, and is set down at the right hand of the throne of God.

The Contagious Faith of One Man.

A few years ago, in a sermon preached by one of my pastors, I was moved to tears by the incredible story of a great man of faith who was stripped of everything he had just because he held onto his faith in Jesus. In the 1800s, a great revival broke out in Wales, England leading to many missionaries traveling to Northeast India to preach the gospel, a province called Assam. This province had residents who were head-hunters and they were aggressive. They didn't welcome the missionaries but one of the missionaries, a Welsh man, was able to successfully win the soul of one man and his family for Christ; an encounter that resulted in other saved souls successfully won for Christ. The village chief was furious as a result of this action. In the presence of the villagers, he told the first family, who got converted, to publicly renounce their faith or face execution. In response to this, the man composed the song:

"I have decided to follow Jesus. I have decided to follow Jesus. I have decided to follow Jesus. No turning back, no turning back."

Infuriated by this, the village chief commanded that the archer shoot the man's two sons and threatened to kill his wife if refuses to denounce his faith in Jesus. The man continued his song:

"Though no one joins me, still I will follow.
Though no one joins me, still I will follow.
Though no one joins me, still I will follow.
No turning back, no turning back."

His wife was shot by the archers at the command of the village chief. Looking at the lifeless bodies of his two children and wife, the man remained resolute, refusing to deny his faith.

The village chief gave the man the opportunity to live if only he can discredit his faith and in his last moments, he concluded the song:

"The cross before me, the world behind me.
The cross before me, the world behind me.
The cross before me, the world behind me.
No turning back, no turning back."

He was shot and he died like every member of his family. This event led to a turnaround in his village. Moved by the faith of this man, the village chief marveled at the great faith that the man and his family exhibited, and he wanted to be part of the faith. The villagers also accepted Christ as their Lord and Savior. **Source: Dr. P.P. Job in 'Why God Why'**

If by one man's faith a village can accept Christ, there is a need for us to be partakers of that faith. I just wonder what would have happened if the man had denied Christ, what would be the fate of the villagers, and the possibility of having this inspirational song and story. The death of this man's children and wife is a great distraction which could have led to the denial of his faith because one would think God should have saved his family from the hands of the village chief but like he concluded his song, the cross before me, the world behind me. He was focusing on what was ahead – Jesus – and forgetting what was behind - the world.

When the driver of the car that hit our car took his eyes off the road and got distracted, it cost him a lot. Although his insurance company will do everything possible for him to get another car, his monthly premium will likely double. When Peter took his eyes off Jesus and was distracted by the waves rolling, he started sinking but he called on the Savior to save him, and, immediately, Jesus stretched His hand to rescue him. Look at Jesus through the windshield, not the rear-view mirror. Zoom in on Jesus through the lens of faith and fear will definitely leave your heart through the back door. Zoom out on fear but zoom in on faith.

CHAPTER 2

Are You Insured?

When my sister reported the accident to the insurance company, they took the damaged car from us because it was a write-off. One of the benefits of having insurance coverage is to give us another car pending when they will finalize the refund processes. We got another car for easy mobility which came at no cost to us because we were covered. At that instance, I just wondered if the car was not insured. We would have had issues with mobility and it's illegal in our province to ride an uninsured car. After a few days, the insurance company valued our car and gave us money to buy another one which also came at no cost to us. Our monthly premium was intact, but the other driver who was at fault had to bear all those costs which will definitely increase his premium. Our damaged car was a 2002 model, but when the insurance company gave us money, we were able to buy a 2005 model car with a great feature called stow and go, an upgrade so to speak. One would not appreciate or understand the value of insurance until you are in a crisis. Many benefits come with a good insurance broker that offers good policies. In this chapter, I will be discussing a few of these benefits that can only be found in the best-rated insurance broker, Jesus. This insurance broker gives you unlimited worldwide coverage irrespective of where you live. It's an eternal coverage with endless value. Someone once stated that "Unless you are immortal, you need life insurance" a statement which I believe to be true. Jesus offers the best insurance policy that will suit your daily and eternal needs. I will give a few details of what He can give you and it's always unlimited depending on the comprehensiveness and depth of your relationship with Him.

Promise of Protection

Isn't it a God-ordained coincidence that Psalm 91:1 is our 9-1-1 call?

He that dwelleth in the secret place of the most High shall abide under the shadow of the Almighty.

The word "dwelleth" means to live permanently. He that dwells in the secret place, not he that wishes to dwell or he who visits the secret place. There are lots of benefits that citizens or permanent residents of a country have access to, but visitors are denied such benefits. In some countries, there is free health care being delivered to those who live permanently and students who are investing through tuition fees in the countries, benefits which are denied to visitors unless they have money to pay which is quite expensive. You can't claim insurance benefits when you have not signed up for the policies or when you are still considering engaging the service of the insurance broker. In order to be covered and protected by God, you need to live and abide in Him. In the scorching sun, we try as much as possible to hide or dwell in a place where the intensity of the sun is, at least, minimized. We have trees that produce shadows under which we rest and feel protected from the heat. The shadow of the Almighty is a place to find eternal rest from every trouble and heat in our lives. This shadow also reminds us that we are never alone in our life's journey when we dwell in the secret place of God. Although we can't see God with our physical eyes, He is forever with us, and His presence abides in us. God's promises to us in Psalms 91 are to deliver us from distress, answer us when we call, honor us, be with us in trouble, give His angels charge over us, show us His salvation, satisfy us with long life and cover us in His feathers. What a robust package! No matter how comprehensive your insurance policy is, it can never be compared to the benefits that God promised us in this chapter of the Bible. Life insurance policies can never promise you a long life, rather they advise you to sign up for life insurance in case of death so that your beneficiaries can have money to fall back on. A man whose breath is in his nostrils needs coverage for his life. I am not against insurance because I have been a beneficiary of insurance coverage, but in addition to the indemnity you have, you need lifelong spiritual security that can only be found in God.

God promised to cover us with his feathers (v. 4) This reminds me of how sensitive and protective mother hens are, their actions sum up motherhood. The mother Hen gets wet while protecting her chicks from rain, thereby keeping them warm. God is more than able to do much more if we abide in Him. A chick that runs out of her mother's wings is exposed to cold and rain. Its life is at great risk and it can be picked by a hawk. The best place to live permanently is at the secret place of the Most High where maximum protection is guaranteed.

Sometimes ago, I carelessly put my cell phone on top of the car while trying to put groceries in the car. I had many things in my hands and I was in a rush not to miss an event. I started driving and didn't realize my phone was still on the roof of the car. I was driving on the road with a speed limit of 80km/hr. Suddenly, I heard a noise and instantly I realized it was my phone that fell off from the roof of the car onto the road with high impact. There were lots of cars coming behind me and I had to stop in the middle of the highway. I ran back to the spot where my phone dropped and I was terrified it would have been broken or crushed by the cars behind me. Fortunately, my phone was intact. However, the phone case was shattered to pieces. I ran back to the car and drove off. Sequel to that event, I didn't have time to get another phone case for my phone. Just a week after, my phone dropped on the floor with a very low impact and the screen got broken leaving huge scars on it. I wondered why my phone didn't break when it fell with a higher impact. The only answer that came to mind was, "It was protected and despite the huge fall, the protector felt the impact but not the phone". God always teaches me life lessons from true-life events. Psalm 91: 1-16 is a great illustration of how God protects and shields His people. Lots of arrows are being shot and attacks are launched at us but we never felt the impact because we dwell under the shelter of the Almighty who is our refuge and our fortress. God is the most valuable and efficient insurance. He gives you unlimited and unrestricted coverage. He has got you covered.

Promise of Confidence

The Lord is my shepherd, I shall not want..... Psalm 23:1-6

David understood what it takes to be a shepherd because he was one before he became a king. When he authored this chapter of the Bible, he was not sharing something vague but something experiential - what a good shepherd does to protect, nurture, and provide for his flocks. David was a shepherd and not just a herdsman. The author did not say, "The Lord is my herdsman, I shall not want" rather he described the Lord as a Shepherd – a shepherd that lays down his life for His flocks. David killed a lion and a bear because of his sheep. He did not only kill the lion but he took the sheep out of the lion's mouth alive. Who does that except one who is willing to sacrifice all for his flock? A herdsman is someone who gets paid for keeping a herd of domesticated animals. One could hardly find someone who will run your business like theirs, a herdsman would most likely not go after the lion or bear because he cannot afford to risk his life for his flock. Sometimes, I imagine how confident the sheep would be when they know that the shepherd is willing to risk his life to protect them. David described the Lord based on what he could relate to. In this modern-day, one can say, The Lord is my Battle Warrior. There are lots of soldiers in different countries fighting and ensuring the peace and safety of millions of people in their countries. They sacrifice their lives, families, and social activities to ensure that millions of lives whose identity they do not know are at peace. How confident are we when we realize some people are at the war front to bring peace and unity to us in the comfort of our homes while going about our daily activities? God has given us confidence that He is our shepherd and all we need to do is to follow His lead because He will never lead us astray. He leads us beside still waters… (v. 2)

Promise of Defense

Just as a lawyer functions as an advocate, advisor, counselor and also represents his or her clients about legal options in court proceedings, so is Jesus our attorney. The devil is known to be the accuser of brethren, one who files a lawsuit against you because of what you did but thank God we have a great defense attorney in Jesus. When the accuser tenders his case in the court of law, you don't need to interfere as the accused, rather you allow your attorney to do his work.

This is a reminder about the scripture in Exodus 14:14 which says, "The Lord will fight for you, and you shall hold your peace." When the Lord fights for you, you don't need to struggle or defend yourself because the battle is His. He has never lost a battle or law case and He will not start with yours. The issue we have most of the time is we try to defend ourselves by negating the importance of our attorney, we end up struggling with it and because the devil is a con man, he knows exactly what to say or do to defeat us. Why not surrender to your attorney and see Him win the case on your behalf? There is something your defense attorney, Jesus, has that the accuser does not have, it's called Grace. Jesus is Grace personified.

How do you sign up for this eternal surety? All you need to do is to forsake your sins and accept Jesus as your Lord and Savior. When Jesus becomes your Lord, He rules in all affairs of your life and you abide in His security. It may sound very simple but it's supernatural.

CHAPTER 3

Follow His Seasons

We have different seasons in a year marked by changes in weather. In some parts of the world, we experience winter, spring, summer, and fall while others experience dry seasons and rainy seasons only. God's creations are diverse and it shows how wide and beautiful the world's canvas can be. To be prepared for the seasons and changes in weather, you need to be acquainted with the seasons. In Canada, where I am based, you are expected to have winter tires or all-season tires in order to be safe during winter because the roads are usually slippery in winter. You can't afford not to have a good winter jacket and boots during winter because they are necessary to keep you warm. Regarding our lives, how prepared are we for each season that comes our way? Do we really know which season is approaching us?

This reminds me of a cold winter morning when I was driving to my sister's place. It was about a 30 minutes drive. It was a foggy day and the clouds were unclear. You could barely see a car 100 meters ahead of you. Although the maximum speed limit designated for the highway was 100km/hr, I had to drive below the speed limit. I noticed that although the traffic light and destination boards were not clear, as I approached these signs, they became clearer. While I couldn't see the cars ahead of me, they got clearer as I drove towards them. I was not driving at a high speed for two reasons, I did not want to hit the cars ahead of me and in case of an emergency stop, I needed to be able to stop at a safe distance. There was no need to rush, I just needed to follow the season and do the needful. While driving, these words came to me, "*Even though I don't know what lies ahead of me while driving, I am still pressing on.*"

This made me reflect on the life of Abraham, who at a time did not have a full plan of what God wanted to do with him, but because he believed the One who knows the ending from the beginning, he entrusted his life and his family into God's hands. He took one step of faith at a time and it was overall credited to him as righteousness. Abraham did not have it altogether but while in a state of "What lies ahead?" He allowed the greatest forerunner to lead him.

It's a very difficult decision to make, being the man of the house, to take your wife, cattle, male, and maid-servants to a land which you do not know. In our present age, if a family wants to relocate to a new location, the man of the house will go and prepare a good place for his family, ensure everything is perfect or close to being perfect before taking his family with him. Every man wants a secure environment for his loved ones. The man may struggle while making the necessary arrangements, but his family will benefit from the sacrifice he made for them and that's a great consolation and achievement on the man's part. In Abraham's case, it was not so. He had to move his family and possessions while heading out from a known place to the unknown. As humans, we all want to know where we are heading to. If a man starts packing and says he is leaving a location, the next question that will come to mind is, "Where are you heading?" and if he can't provide a definitive answer as to where he is heading, he will be seen as an unserious person. If you are leaving a location, you must have a destination. No man walks into an airport and says I need to board a plane that is heading somewhere. You need a destination. I assume most people would have mocked Abraham when they asked him where he was heading and he replied that he was heading wherever God showed him. It was a great call. God could have told him where he was heading before he left Haran, but God is a God of season and process. Abraham believed in God for the fulfillment of the promises to make him a great nation and a blessing to the world, but the process was not revealed to him.

In Genesis 12:1 -5, the Bible says:

Now the Lord had said unto Abram, Get thee out of thy country, and from thy kindred, and from thy father's house, unto a land that I will shew thee: And I will make of thee a great nation, and I will bless thee, and make thy name great; and thou shalt be a blessing: And I will bless them that bless thee, and curse him that curseth thee: and in thee shall all families of the earth be blessed. So Abram departed, as the Lord had spoken unto him; and Lot went with him: and Abram was seventy and five years old when he departed out of Haran. And Abram took Sarai, his wife, and Lot his brother's son, and all their substance that they had gathered, and the souls that they had gotten in Haran; and they went forth to go into the land of Canaan; and into the land of Canaan they came.

Our pursuit to know God's will for our lives is a call to faith and dependence on God. God does not reveal the whole plan and process to us, He wants us to take one step at a time while trusting Him, the Master Planner. Most times, by following what God has revealed or told us, He reveals the next level. A teacher will not reveal the curriculum of the next academic year to you simply because he knows you would take the class.

Jesus described one who is the greatest in the Kingdom as someone who is like a child that is totally dependent on his/her parents. For example, if you tell a little child to get into the car for a ride to an ice cream shop, he or she would be totally dependent on you to bear the cost. As adults, we often think we are smart enough to know everything and where things will result based on our experience, but God wants us to be totally dependent on Him.

Matthew 18:1-4

At the same time came the disciples unto Jesus, saying, Who is the greatest in the kingdom of heaven? And Jesus called a little child unto him, and set him in the midst of them, And said, Verily I say unto you, Except ye be converted, and become as little children, ye shall not enter into the kingdom of heaven. Whosoever therefore shall humble himself as this little child, the same is greatest in the kingdom of heaven.

You don't have to know the process or everything about your life before you start acting on the Word. God who has brought you this far didn't consult you before bringing you to this present state in your life. Don't try to wrap your head around God's revelation, it's far beyond our human reasoning. Heeding God's call takes us out of our comfort zone and stability, but how well do we depend on God to lead us on his path to an expected end that he has prepared us for? God sometimes calls a person to leave his job and go into ministry, calls another to leave his location and go to missionary field, and others to give their valued treasure to the poor; and to depend on him. Many times, God wants to reveal our weaknesses to us by making us go through some phases just to reveal that we are not self-sufficient. If we can trust pilots and sailors with our lives, how much more God? If you board a flight to Heathrow Airport, London and on your way, the pilot states your present location or decides to take another route to London because of bad weather on the regular route, you still trust that they will take you to our final destination safely.

In Genesis 22, God told Abraham to sacrifice his beloved son, Isaac, as a burnt sacrifice. God did not request for Ishmael but Isaac. Abraham obeyed God's instruction and he embarked on a journey to the region of Moriah on a mountain God planned to show him. On getting there, Abraham told his two servants to stay behind with the donkey while he and Isaac go and worship after which they will both return.

Genesis 22:4-5

On the third day Abraham looked up and saw the place in the distance. He said to his servants, "Stay here with the donkey while I and the boy go over there. We will worship and then we will come back to you."

Did Abraham lie about his return with Isaac who was the sacrificial lamb? No, he didn't lie about it. Although Abraham did not know about God's full plan, he trusted God to unfold his plans as he obeys. This unwavering trust in God persisted when

Isaac asked his father about the sacrificial lamb. Abraham knew Isaac was the sacrificial lamb according to God's instruction, but Abraham still believed God to provide. And God did provide a ram for the burnt sacrifice instead of Isaac. Abraham called the name of the place "The Lord will provide". God begins to unfold His master plan when we follow His seasons and trust Him even when we do not have the full knowledge of His plan. A long path becomes clearer as you approach, likewise, a long-distance becomes shorter when you move closer following the right directions. Learn to trust God and walk in His seasons.

CHAPTER 4

Restraint

Your physical safety is important likewise your spiritual safety. It is compulsory to buckle your seatbelt properly to avoid injury in case of an accident. It is also important to have child restraint in a moving car for safety. Although most of the kids I know don't like being restrained in a car seat, for safety purposes, whether they like it or not, you have to buckle them properly. This brings us to the armor of God. The Bible says, "Put on the whole armor of God" not "Trust God to put it on you". Safety is your responsibility. In life, we have some responsibilities which God will not take for us and others can't help us with them solely because they are ours to take. We are to put on the whole armor of God, not a few of them. The Bible made us understand that this world is a battleground and as soldiers of Christ, we need to put on the full armor of God. A typical Roman soldier would have his armor on when he goes to the battlefield. Ever wondered why Saul gave his armor to David in preparation to fight Goliath? In order to be an overcomer in the battle against the wiles of the devil, we need to have our full armor on. Although the physical armor was mentioned in the Bible, while reflecting on Saul, Ahab, and Goliath's armor you will realize that these armors are limited and cannot be used as a defense in spiritual battles. Saul's armor was too big for David and although Saul had armor, he couldn't face Goliath. Goliath's armor was useless with David's stone and a stray arrow penetrated king Ahab's armor which led to his death. All these depict that spiritual armors are needed to fight the battles since our warfare is not carnal. In this chapter, we will discuss the whole armor of God and How we can put them on for a successful and victorious battle.

Belt of Truth

This holds all the other pieces of armor in place. The truth of the scripture is against the lies of the devil, for he is the father of lies. The truth is about the love of God and what God has done for us through Christ. The devil wants us to believe that we are not loved and God is angry with us but the good news is that our deliverance lies in the truth of God's Word.

John 8:32 NIV

"Then you will know the truth, and the truth will set you free.

One of Satan's greatest tactics is to trade his lies for the truth we have or know, beware of his schemes. God does not only want us to know the truth, He wants us to live it, walk in it, and embrace it. It is possible to know the truth but shy away from it. It's so surprising how some Christians know the Word of God which is the sword of the Spirit but without the belt of truth, this leads them to make fatal conclusions in life. When Jesus was led to the wilderness to be tempted by the devil, Jesus overcame him because He is the way, the truth, and the life. The devil quoted Psalm 91:11-12 "*For he shall give his angels charge over thee, to keep thee in all thy ways. They shall bear thee up in their hands, lest thou dash thy foot against a stone*". Of course, these are the words of the

Lord but is it applicable to yielding to Satan's temptation? No! Jesus replied with the truth that supports this word, *"It is said: 'Do not put the Lord your God to the test.'"* Why would you intentionally take poison and quote scriptures that it will not harm you? It is one thing to know the Word of God, but it's also important to live it by wearing Christ who is truth personified. Remember, God's Word is true but the devil can manipulate you with the Word of God and if you don't know the truth of the Word and its application, you can fall into the devil's pit.

Breastplate of Righteousness

Jesus is righteousness personified so he could confidently say that the prince of this world has nothing in Him. God wants us to walk in this righteousness that Jesus has given freely to us when we confessed Him as our Lord and Saviour. Unrighteousness gives Satan a stronghold in the lives of those who practice it. The breastplate covers and shields the heart and vital organs from being attacked likewise the righteousness of Christ Jesus. We do not earn it as a result of our good deed but we are yoked with the righteousness that comes with salvation which protects us from Satan's accusations and charges.

Romans 3:10
As it is written: "There is none righteous, no, not one.

2 Corinthians 5:21
For He made Him who knew no sin to be sin for us, that we might become the righteousness of God in Him.

Ephesians 2:8
For by grace you have been saved through faith, and that not of yourselves; it is the gift of God,

Philippians 3:9
And be found in Him, not having my own righteousness, which is from the law, but that which is through faith in Christ, the righteousness which is from God by faith;

The only means to experience victory in the battle against Satan is through confidence that the righteousness of Jesus has got us covered, otherwise condemnation sets in, and it could lead to failure or destruction.

Shoes of the Gospel of Peace

Who can walk barefoot on broken glasses or a waste landfill? Good shoes are required on the battleground. As soldiers of Christ, the shoes of the gospel of peace are necessary in order to walk on the path that Jesus trod. There may be obstacles on our paths thrown by adversaries, but the shoes of peace make us less sensitive to their oppositions by focusing more on steps to move forward and win the battle we are fighting. With the shoes of the gospel of peace, we can advance with the gospel and remain focused on our forerunner and not backslide therefore bringing many sons to God.

Isaiah 52:7
How beautiful upon the mountains
Are the feet of him who brings good news,

Who proclaims peace,
Who brings glad tidings of good things,
Who proclaims salvation,
Who says to Zion,
"Your God reigns!"

Shield of Faith

Faith is the opposite of fear. Those who go to the battlefield with fear in their heart end up being destroyed at the war front. When Gideon was about to go on a battle with the Midianites, he summoned his men. 32,000 people showed up but God instructed him to announce to his army that anyone who trembles in fear should turn back and leave Mount Gilead. Surprisingly, 22, 000 men turned back which is about 68.75% of the men who showed up. One of the schemes of the devil is fear. Fear is the devil's greatest weapon with which he penetrates through the heart of men. Satan sends darts of fear to bring doubt but we have the greatest weapon to conquer him - our faith in Jesus. David had faith in God to conquer Goliath even without the physical armor given to him by King Saul. I want to believe that Satan would have talked David out of his adventure to fight Goliath but a man of faith overcomes every dart of the devil. Goliath had given his words that if an Israelite was able to defeat him, the philistines will become the Israelites' subject but if otherwise, the Israelites will be their subjects. With such threats, the people of Israel and King Saul became terrified, the devil was already successful by engulfing the Israelites with fear but David was different, he was able to throw back the darts of fear with his spiritual shield. A man who is set to do a work of faith will most likely be obstructed which is why he needs a shield of faith. David acted out in boldness and valor because he believed God was with him to fight the battle and we all know the result - Satan's dart of fear and doubt glanced off the shield of faith. Satan knows there is power in the faith you exercise, and that it can produce good results which is why he is always attacking our faith by sending fear. Remember, anytime the devil brings fear, he knows you already have the faith to bring your expectations to life. Don't you ever quit on your faith rather quit on fear and exercise your faith. Goliath's stature and weapons were capable of arresting the heart of David but faith sees possibilities even in dead situations. By faith, David put a stone in his slingshot and hurled it towards Goliath and the rest was a victorious history. Goliath threatened but David spoke the words of faith, and it was as David has said because his words were not empty words but victorious and affirmative words backed up with faith.

1 Samuel 17: 45-47

"David said to the Philistine, "You come against me with sword and spear and javelin, but I come against you in the name of the Lord Almighty, the God of the armies of Israel, whom you have defied. This day the Lord will deliver you into my hands, and I'll strike you down and cut off your head. This very day I will give the carcasses of the Philistine army to the birds and the wild animals, and the whole world will know that there is a God in Israel. All those gathered here will know that it is not by sword or spear that the Lord saves; for the battle is the Lord's, and he will give all of you into our hands."

Faith has dimensions. As we walk with God closely, our faith grows. At the end of Paul's life he wrote:

2 Timothy 4:7
I have fought a good fight, I have finished my course, I have kept the faith.

Life is a battlefield and we have to fight the battle with the arsenal God has given us, but it is our responsibility to put them on for a guaranteed victory.

Helmet of Salvation

Ever wonder why helmets are included in the equipment needed to protect users from health or safety risks in some occupations or those riding motorbikes and bicycles? It is hard and it reduces the impact on the head giving resistance to anything that targets the head. When we have the sure knowledge of our salvation, we won't be moved by Satan's deception. After Jesus' baptism, the heavens were opened, and the Spirit of God descended like a dove on Jesus. A voice from heaven said, "This is my beloved Son, in whom I am well pleased." These are practical experiences affirming Jesus' identity as the Messiah sent from Heaven to liberate us. Just after this encounter, the devil tempted Jesus by showing him all the kingdoms of this world and promised to give all to Jesus if Jesus would worship him. Jesus knew that no one is worthy of His worship except the Father and He had the knowledge of who he is - the son of God. He was able to counter the devil's manipulative words to turn the stone to bread if truly he is the son of God. This is how Satan works. If you don't have the knowledge of who you are in Christ and the benefits of salvation, he will manipulate you by trading lies with you in exchange for the truth. Jesus knew he was the son of God, no doubt about that, but the devil was trying to manipulate Jesus so that He would probably doubt his identity as the son of God when God has already affirmed His identity. This is deception! The helmet of

salvation helps us protect our thoughts so that our head is not open to everything and anything the devil is raining down.

1 Thessalonians 5:8
But let us, who are of the day, be sober, putting on the breastplate of faith and love; and for an helmet, the hope of salvation.

Sword of the Spirit

This is the Word of God which is powerful. Don't go to the battle ground empty because your oppositions have weapons and are also battle-ready. This is the only spiritual armor that is defensive and offensive.

Hebrews 4:12
For the word of God is living and powerful, and sharper than any two-edged sword, piercing even to the division of soul and spirit, and of joints and marrow, and is a discerner of the thoughts and intents of the heart.

When the devil tempted Jesus with the scriptures, Jesus answered with "It is written" Jesus was word personified, he had the right weapon to use at the right time. What weapon do you have to attack your adversaries? The Word of God gives us life and revelation of God. The Sword of the Spirit can be used against the enemy and it is also effective for personal use. The Word of God liberates us from captivity, and it also becomes reality in our lives when we follow it. There are no limits to what the sword of the Spirit can do for us. It is truth, lamp, and light to us depending on our revelation of it.

With all the arsenal we have, we need to soak ourselves and these armor in prayers. Prayer brings us into communion and intimacy with God for protection. The whole armor of God will empower us to be strong in the Lord and the power of His might because we are comprehensively secured from all attacks from our adversaries. Remember to put on the whole armor because putting on the helmet of salvation without the shield of faith may result in fiery darts penetrating our hearts.

How Do We Put on the Armor of God?

Romans 13: 14
But put on the Lord Jesus Christ, and make no provision for the flesh, to fulfill its lusts.

By giving your life to Jesus, you have the opportunity of clothing yourself with the full or whole armor of God which comes with salvation.

CHAPTER 5

Spiritual Gauge

I remember while growing up, we always travel on vacation as a family. We go by road and the excitement of traveling to a bigger city for my siblings and me is indescribable. Most times my dad drives while my mom and my siblings enjoy the ride. I rarely sleep the night before taking off because of the excitement. I love sightseeing and most times, I don't eat before we take off because I know we always grab a few items once we get to some specific places to rest. One thing I remember my dad has never failed to do is filling up his gas tank before we take off on any journey. In African countries, we do not have self-serve options. My dad will always tell the pump operator, "Fill up" but I couldn't endure the time taken to fill up the tank, all I wanted was for us to start heading to our destination. I always thought to myself, why not buy little then we can buy more once we leave our city? I never thought or understood the possibility of running out of gas and how devastating it could get. Some time ago, I went grocery shopping with my sister and I had to drive her car. I didn't check the gas gauge of the car before leaving her place, we went to different stores and we finally got home. Later in the evening, I wanted to go to church with her car. I started the ignition and tried to drive out of her driveway. While reversing, the car stopped. I tried starting the ignition again but it never worked. I called my brother-in-law to help check the car, he came out to check the car and he said, "You are out of gas." I started lamenting but the warning sound of the gas tank never went off, I didn't hear anything. He said you have to check the gas gauge and the warning light will always pop up to notify you about a low level of gas. I had to move the car from where it was because it was obstructing the cars coming on that side of the road. Immediately, I called Uber to take me to the nearest gas station, on getting there, I wanted to get at least a 10-liter gallon to buy gas but the cashier said they ran out of the bigger gallon. I was able to purchase a small gallon that could contain about 5-6 liters of gas. I then took Uber to my sister's residence to pour the gas into the gas tank which was sufficient to get me to the gas station before buying more. All these happened on a cold winter evening. I was already freezing by the time I was done filling the gas tank. I was able to drive back to the driveway but was already late for the church service. The first thing that came to my mind while I was reflecting on the incident was "WISDOM". If I had checked the gas gauge to know the level of gas in the car, I would have saved myself the stress which I had to go through. I did what I was supposed to do at the wrong time which resulted in stress, waste of resources, and absence from church. Now nobody needs to tell me why my dad would fill his gas tank before heading out. I learned my lesson a hard way but I believe it always reminds me to do the needful at the right time. Ever asked yourself how far you can drive on an empty gas tank? When the gas level reaches the reserve fuel level, do you ignore the gas warning light which pops up? or you don't check your gas level before starting the car? This story is similar to the parable of the 10 virgins in the Bible. Like the 5 wise virgins, how spiritually prepared are you? Let us look at the similarities between the 5 wise virgins and the 5 foolish virgins. They are all virgins with lamps. They all took their lamps to meet the bridegroom. They all fell asleep while waiting for the bridegroom. At midnight when the cry rang out about the arrival of the bridegroom, they all woke up and trimmed their lamps. The only thing that distinguished the wise virgins from the foolish virgins was the preparation. Although the foolish virgins made efforts to buy oil so their lamps won't go out, it was too late. While they were on their way to get extra oil, the bridegroom arrived and those who were ready for the bridegroom went to the banquet with him while the door was shut at the foolish virgins upon arrival. The foolish virgins could have thought that the bridegroom would arrive soon enough before their lamps ran out of oil but their prediction was wrong. Life happens and we can't really determine when something will occur but we need to be prepared. If you get 10 liters of gas with the hope that you are traveling a short distance, what would you do if you miss your way or if unforeseen circumstances arise and you have to take a longer route to your destination, your gas will not double in quantity but it will run out with distance. I believe most people can relate to these stories based on their past experiences in life. There are instances where we get late to some events and we realize that we would have been involved in many enjoyable activities if not for our lateness. A student who goes to the exam hall late is not likely to be accepted. However, if he/she is accepted to partake in the exam, he will not get the same time as other students because he/she has missed some of the apportioned time for the exam. So here is the important question you should ask yourself, Am I spiritually prepared? For centuries, they have been proclaiming these words, "Jesus Christ is coming soon!" Generations keep passing it on, but the bridegroom is still not here. Are you losing your oil or do you have extra oil to last you till the arrival of the bridegroom?

The kind of oil that is needed to illuminate the way and light up the darkness is not shareable… In our lives, the oil of preparedness is accumulated drop by drop in righteous living… Each act of dedication and obedience is a drop added to our store.

President Spencer W. Kimball, *Faith precedes the miracle. Shadow mountain publishing.*

We can't share our spiritual oil with others but we can teach them how and where to get theirs. Spiritual preparedness allows us to patiently await the arrival of the bridegroom, Jesus Christ. While the righteous eagerly awaits this arrival, to the wicked, it's dreaded news that judgment day is at hand.

Matthew 25:13
Therefore keep watch, because you do not know the day or the hour.

No one knows the hour or the day of the second coming of Jesus Christ, while we await His arrival, we should be earthly useful by being ready through consistent trimming and burning of our lamps. We cannot afford to run out of oil. We need to daily reflect on the parable of the 10 virgins and mirror ourselves in the Word of God to ensure we are living like the 5 wise virgins and not the foolish ones.

"The oil of preparedness and steadiness is accumulated each day through consistent, wise choices. ... Deliberate, consistent, and reliable preparation and performance provide essential oil for our lamps."

David A. Bednar, *New Era, Jan 2008 © Intellectual Reserve, Inc. All rights reserved.*

How Do We Prepare for the Second Coming of Christ?

With faith and hope in Jesus that He is coming again, we get motivated to keep trusting in His words about His second arrival. Preparation for the arrival of the bridegroom is a continuous process that involves faithfulness, praying (both in and out of seasons), obedience to God's commands, righteous living, seeking to have the revelation of Christ, true worship, love for others, sacrifices, meditating on the Word of God, living a purposeful life and above all, the infilling of the Holy Spirit which guides and inspires us to fulfill all we need to do while anticipating the arrival of our bridegroom. It is an individual responsibility to ensure our lamp is burning and that we have extra oil to keep us going in our journey in life. We can't share our oil with others not because we are selfish but because it's unshareable. I have never shared my toothbrush with anyone, not my children or spouse. It's not due to selfishness but each of us needs to have our toothbrush for sanitary reasons. So, if you want to help someone to keep their lamps burning, show them where to get extra oil - the source is God. Do not procrastinate the day of your repentance or salvation because it may be too late which will cost you immensely. Remember the 5 foolish virgins were at the venue waiting for the arrival of the bridegroom but had to leave to get extra oil. I never imagined the car would run out of gas, but when it did, all the effort to get more gas was stressful and I couldn't meet up with the important evening church service I was meant to attend. Don't ever think you can predict His arrival, it may be at the hour you least expected. How prepared are you?

CHAPTER 6

Blind Spots

In some countries of the world, blind spots in driving are not often mentioned because drivers are trained to rely on rear or side-view mirrors to see vehicles coming up on their side. However, this has resulted in lots of accidents which mostly claimed lives. My knowledge of blind spots in driving has saved me a few times from crashing into another vehicle which I didn't see using rear-view or side mirrors, but I was able to see the cars by shoulder checking and through the help of passengers riding with me in the car. A blind spot is not a word you would likely see in the Bible, however we can relate some real life lessons to the kingdom principles to learn and better understand the scriptures. A spiritual blindspot is an area or areas of our lives which affects us negatively but most times we choose to ignore them because they have a minute impact or due to our ignorance. Most times as a passenger in a car, I always ensure I check blind spot areas for the driver because I had received the help of my passengers which saved me from wrecking my car and that of others. People can help us identify the spiritual blind spot in our lives, nevertheless we need to have a teachable spirit so we can heed to the Holy Spirit speaking through them.

Galatians 6:1-5

Brothers and sisters, if someone is caught in a sin, you who live by the Spirit should restore that person gently. But watch yourselves, or you also may be tempted. Carry each other's burdens, and in this way you will fulfill the law of Christ. If anyone thinks they are something when they are not, they deceive themselves. Each one should test their own actions. Then they can take pride in themselves alone, without comparing themselves to someone else, for each one should carry their own load.

I love the word *gently* as used in the above scripture. Most times when we talk to people about their ungodly characters, the approach and attitude go a long way in helping them mirror themselves in the light of God's Word. You don't want to attack them by rubbing their bad deeds on their faces. Some of them are ashamed of what they have done so the last thing they need is someone attacking them when they are already guilty of their sins. It is important to know that honor goes a long way when speaking to people, especially when you are ministering to them to turn from their old ways. You need to deal with them gently.

David was a man after God's heart but he had blind spots. David knew he was about to commit adultery with Bathsheba, Uriah's wife, but he suppressed the thoughts and went further till he commanded that Uriah be sent to the front lines of battle where David knew he would be killed. This act was to cover up for his sins. David could have thought that no one knew about his motive and that, as a king, he might not get any punishment for his actions. God saw everything that happened and because David was a man after

God's heart, God wanted him to repent but it took someone's help to bring David to the realization of his blindspot.

2 Samuel 12:1-7

The Lord sent Nathan to David. When he came to him, he said, "There were two men in a certain town, one rich and the other poor. The rich man had a very large number of sheep and cattle, but the poor man had nothing except one little ewe lamb he had bought. He raised it, and it grew up with him and his children. It shared his food, drank from his cup and even slept in his arms. It was like a daughter to him. "Now a traveler came to the rich man, but the rich man refrained from taking one of his own sheep or cattle to prepare a meal for the traveler who had come to him. Instead, he took the ewe lamb that belonged to the poor man and prepared it for the one who had come to him."

David burned with anger against the man and said to Nathan, "As surely as the Lord lives, the man who did this must die! He must pay for that lamb four times over, because he did such a thing and had no pity."

Then Nathan said to David, "*You are the man! This is what the Lord, the God of Israel, says: 'I anointed you king over Israel, and I delivered you from the hand of Saul.* Nathan's approach was guided by God's wisdom. He understood what honor meant so he didn't condemn David by attacking him with what he had done, rather his approach made David condemn his own actions without Nathan judging him.

2 Samuel 12: 13
Then David said to Nathan, "I have sinned against the Lord." Nathan replied, "The Lord has taken away your sin. You are not going to die.

God wants us to be conscious of what we have done and his desire is for us to repent from our evil ways. God is aware of our wrong deeds and when we seek His forgiveness, that's the time we become true with ourselves by taking responsibility for our actions. God is forever merciful and full of unfailing love because Jesus is Grace and Love personified. We need to be humble enough to believe that we are prone to errors and when we do, we should believe in the forgiving power of God and also understand that no sin is greater than the other. It's a sin no matter its magnitude.

"If you and I can't think of the last time we were wrong, something is really wrong. We are losing our grip of reality." Beth Moore

David was not trying to vindicate himself, rather he made a plea for God's help to discern his blind spots when he wrote;

Psalm 19:12
"But who can discern their own errors? Forgive my hidden faults.

This reinforces the fact that we need God's help to unveil those hidden sins we may not pay attention to or those we overlook as minute because they do not have damaging results yet. The Holy Spirit is the One who brings to our consciousness the faults in us by convicting us according to the Biblical instructions.

Psalm 139: 23-24
Search me, God, and know my heart;
test me and know my anxious thoughts.
See if there is any offensive way in me,
and lead me in the way everlasting.

There are different types of blind spots in our lives and some of them have Biblical characters that better explain these issues. In this book, I will discuss five blind spots.

1. Defiance - Pharaoh demonstrated what could be described as open resistance to God's warnings and instructions to let the Israelites go. Despite the plagues that befell the Egyptians, Pharaoh's heart was hardened and he was not willing to let go. Just like Pharaoh, there are some hard habits we are not willing to let go of due to the rigidity of our hearts but in the long run, these habits lead to destruction. I am not disputing the fact that we have to be rigid with some decisions in our lives, nonetheless, there are some habits that we need to be flexible enough to release to make life easier for us. Some of these ugly lifestyles affect those around us and not just us. God sent 10 different plagues to the Egyptians, although most of them were not involved in the decision made by Pharaoh, they were partakers of the perdition. Plagues were not enough to break Pharaoh, so he ended up in the red sea with his armies. Many families in Egypt were hurt due to one man's disobedience to God's instructions. Pharaoh never acknowledged his blindspot, hence he was destroyed alongside many families. Most of our blind spots have lasting effects on the people around us. While some of the people in our circle of influence are bold to point it out to us, many of these people will have to live with these issues hurting on the inside. What would it cost Pharaoh to let go of the Israelites? What would it cost you also to acknowledge your blindspot and let go so that you will enjoy peace and those around you can live at peace with you. The solution to defiance is willingness but are you willing to let go?

2. Haughty entitlement - Judas Iscariot, one of the twelve disciples chosen by Jesus, misused his position and it resulted in self-destruction. At times, we indulge in things that we feel make us comfortable not minding how they affect the people in our lives. Judas Iscariot betrayed Jesus because of thirty silver coins. Selfishness breeds betrayal. Judas asked the chief priest what he was willing to give him if he hands over Jesus to them. Jesus has been with the disciples for a few years and one would think that as a disciple and treasure of Jesus, Judas would be loyal to his master but his loyalty lied with others. While at the Lord's supper, Jesus said, One of you will betray me. One after the other they said to him, Surely not I, Lord! This should have served as an eye-opener for Judas that Jesus already knew what was to come and at that time he had the opportunity to refund the money to the chief priest and amend his ways, but his arrogance and selfish interest would not allow him despite Jesus pointing out this blindspot. Jesus further said, Woe to the man who betrays the Son of Man, it would be better for him if he had not been born. All these meant nothing to Judas, he pressed further to fulfill his mission. There is a saying that "To be forewarned is to be forearmed" that is, knowledge or warning in advance helps you to better prepare for what is coming. It's so heartbreaking when we have a warning ahead and we fall into the pit which we knew existed, what then would have happened if we were not notified ahead of time? Remember, Judas also said to Jesus, Surely not I, Rabbi! But Jesus answered, Yes, it is you. At times, I wonder what Jesus' response meant to Judas. Did he just ignore that red alert? This statement sounds like a fire alarm that just went off in a house, the residents of the house will be worried until the sound is resolved. This is not an ordinary statement, Yes, it is you who will betray me. After Jesus' betrayal, Judas went to hang himself. Surprisingly, he died before Jesus. Jesus would have still died because our salvation lies in His death and resurrection, but being betrayed by someone you love is heartbreaking.

3. Indignation - Have you ever been treated unjustly and it has resulted in bitterness and deep hurt? I can identify with you but this is the truth; bitterness is a biohazard material, which is poisonous to you and those in your lives. Although it may feel justifiable from your perspective, it is not God's way. God didn't want us to experience what the old testament people faced, hence He sacrificed His only Son to reconcile us back to Him. What is justifiable is this, sinners should face the consequences of their actions (an eye for an eye, a tooth for a tooth) but God sent Grace-personified to us so that we don't have to sacrifice animals for the atonement of our sins. Jesus' blood took away the bitterness and betrayal while He gave us eternal life and peace with God. What amazing love! People don't have to go through what you went through in life, rather you can be an extended arm of God to them so that their journey will be with ease, free of pain and in so doing, you have become a blessing to them. Forgiveness is key to indignation and resentment. Let go of every bitterness and hurt. Allow God to heal you and bring the best out of your scars.

4. Segregation - What happens when we isolate ourselves from those who can point out our blind spot and also help us? It could result in fatality. Many times, we feel those who correct us are the wrong people while those who embrace all our characters are the best people we need in our lives. Those who correct us seek to bring out the best in us, while those who accept everything we do most often hurt inside as a result of our attitude but they are unable to point it to us because they feel the outcome will not be favorable.

Proverbs 27:6
Wounds from a friend can be trusted,
but an enemy multiplies kisses.

We should never segregate ourselves from those who correct us. We are unable to see our blind spots but others who see them and know the danger they could bring to us and our loved ones are in a better position to warn us to avoid perdition. Oftentimes, we perceive the world as unsafe as well as the people in it, however, some great people are safe and reliable enough to surround ourselves with. Have you heard the saying, "No man is an island?" It means no man is self-sufficient. You will always need someone around you to help in the journey of life. I have learned that When God wants to bless you, He uses humans, and on the other hand, if Satan wants to torment someone he uses humans. Humans are necessities in our lives but with God's help and spiritual sensitivity we will be able to walk with and surround ourselves with those God has brought our ways to be a blessing to us and not instruments of destruction. The best person who can navigate through life with you is the Holy Spirit. You constantly need intimacy with Him because to live successfully in life's journey, He is one friend you can never live without.

5. Deliberate ignorance - I have heard some people say, "I know it's not the best decision but that is what I want to do and I am sticking to it." It's so surprising how we are deliberately rigid on ignorance. One thing we fail to understand is that by deliberate ignorance, we lie to ourselves by ignoring the reality of the circumstance either due to fear or low self-esteem.

Psalm 119:29 (NLT)
Keep me from lying to myself; give me the privilege of knowing your instructions.

Just as it is possible to have faith during chaos, it is possible to lie to oneself when everything does not look like what God has promised. Knowledge is light, however applied knowledge is power. Walk in the true knowledge and be deliberate in obeying the signals and instructions that will guide you into safety.

In conclusion, to overcome spiritual blind spots, we must constantly mirror ourselves in the Word of God which will bring our blind spots to the open.

CHAPTER 7

The Drowsy Driver

It has been proven that drowsy driving slows reaction time, reduces vigilance, and impairs information processing. Why then do we have sleepy drivers knowing the risk and the consequences involved? The rate at which fatal accidents occur as a result of sleeping is quite alarming. I strongly believe that no one would get on the bus or plane that is being controlled by a sleepy driver or pilot if you got the information beforehand because it's not safe. Every driver, pilot, sailor, and loco pilot has to be in their right frame of mind with the ability to process information accurately and to also make safety decisions in case of an emergency. Likewise spiritually, in our journey in life, we need to be vigilant and alert to sail through the storms of life without our ship capsizing. How then do we make great decisions when we are not aware of our surroundings or what lies ahead? This is a wake-up call to all citizens of heaven whose desire is to live unharmed and excellently well on earth and to also triumphantly transit to heaven at the end of their journey here on earth.

Sleep can be divided into two groups; physical sleep and spiritual sleep. Physical sleep is important for everyone to feel refreshed, grow, and be alive. It is one of the activities we have to partake in as humans. It's biblical to sleep because God gives us dreams in our sleep. Every human being sleeps every day, however the average sleeping time differs with each person. Surprisingly, it's not everyone that sleeps spiritually because it is dangerous and could be deadly.

Matthew 13:25
But while men slept, his enemy came and sowed tares among the wheat and went his way.

The above scripture made us understand that the wheat was already planted which means something great has been sown on fertile land which these men were supposed to be vigilant to watch and nurture but because they slept off, the enemy came to sow tares; an injurious weed that resembles wheat when young. These men were deeply asleep such that they were not aware of the time the enemy came, when he sowed the tares, and when he left. A weed is an unwanted grass growing in an unwanted area that could inhibit the growth of the intended seed. Unlike every other weed, tares resemble wheat when they are young. This weed was not noticed early until the wheat grain sprouted and the tares appeared. I want to believe the servants were shocked when they saw the tares growing with the wheat. What are these? When were the tares planted? We thought they were wheat. These men were not sure about what was rightly planted.

Matthew 13:27
So the servants of the owner came and said to him, 'Sir, did you not sow good seed in your field? How then does it have tares?'

One of the dangers of spiritual drowsiness is confusion and if wrong decisions were made, it could lead to total destruction. While the servants asked if they could gather up the tares, the master declined because he knew they could uproot the wheat alongside the tares which could lead to the destruction of the whole plant. The wheat had to grow with the tares although it wasn't convenient, it could have been avoided if the men were awake to monitor the wheat.

The enemy is always alert, and knows the best time to strike - when men sleep. While asleep, you are unprepared for what is coming. Also, you are not aware of what the enemy is doing because you are in a completely relaxed state. In the physical world, battles are lost as a result of some people's unpreparedness while disaster has struck many homes and places while men slept. If all these could happen in the world where we live, it's an indication that we need to know the dangers that lie in spiritual drowsiness and how to avoid them. I will examine five different examples in the Bible that I have tagged syndromes because they are all characterized by an associated symptom called spiritual drowsiness.

The Jonah syndrome

God commanded Jonah to go preach to the people of Nineveh but he boarded a ship sailing towards Tarshish, another direction. While onboard, God sent a great wind on the sea and each sailor started calling on their gods to save them, but Jonah was deeply asleep on the deck. The captain went down to Jonah and entreated him to call on his God to save them.

Jonah 1:5-6

All the sailors were afraid and each cried out to his own god. And they threw the cargo into the sea to lighten the ship.

But Jonah had gone below deck, where he lay down and fell into a deep sleep. The captain went to him and said, "How can you sleep? Get up and call on your god! Maybe he will take notice of us so that we will not perish."

Spiritually, as far as our souls are concerned, many of us are deeply asleep in the midst of the violent storm caused either by life's turbulence or sin. Just like Jonah was comfortably relaxed in the tempest, some people are comfortable with their sinful life and the danger that comes with it. The Captain told Jonah to call on his God for their safety, but Jonah refrained. No matter the situation we find ourselves in, we should not be ashamed or guilty of calling on God who can bring us out of the pit because at that point in time, we are helpless. Wallowing in the ocean of sin for a very long time can lead us to a deep ocean current which could be disastrous. While Jonah failed to call on God in a place of safety – the ship – he called on God in great distress in the belly of a fish. I have never lived in the belly of a fish, but I am very sure it's more comfortable to be in a ship than to live in a fish for three days and three nights. Just like a sequoia tree grows from seed to being one of the skyscrapers of the natural world, so does sin grows into uncontrollable events. We should never allow ourselves to be swallowed up before we seek salvation. God is ever waiting on us to wake up from our sleep or slumber and to rise from the darkness into the light of Christ.

Ephesians 5:14

Therefore He says: "Awake, you who sleep, Arise from the dead, And Christ will give you light.

The disciple syndrome

Jesus had informed His disciples earlier that He would suffer in the hands of the religious leaders and that He would be betrayed by one of His own. While in the garden of Gethsemane, Jesus went a little farther away from His disciples to pray and He instructed them to sit and keep watch with Him, but unfortunately the disciples were deeply asleep. On his first return, He gave them instructions to stay alert; be in prayer so you won't wander in temptation and the danger that lies ahead. Jesus knew what would happen to his disciples after His arrest that was why he told them to pray but they were exhausted and their eyes were heavy with sleep. Some Christians are like the disciples, spiritually worn out and exhausted while they are expected to be active. We always need to watch and pray because the enemy attacks at our weakest moments. Just like Jesus commanded His disciples to watch and pray. As Christians, we need to be alert because the enemies will not inform us before they attack, that is why we cannot afford to be spiritually worn out. Many dangerous things creep into our lives when we are spiritually drained because we are not vigilant. Your enemy never sleeps, neither should you sleep spiritually.

1 Peter 5:8 (The Message)
Keep a cool head. Stay alert. The Devil is poised to pounce, and would like nothing better than to catch you napping. Keep your guard up.

The Samson syndrome

We are familiar with the story of Samson the Great and the influence of Delilah in his fall. Delilah had asked Samson about the source of his strength thrice but Samson gave her fictitious answers which failed after Delilah's attempt. There is a high possibility of you falling into unconscious spiritual sleep as a result of being unequally yoked with the wrong people or things that entice you and look glittery, not knowing the bitterness loaded in such people or things. This is the reason why our spiritual eyes need to be alert and vigilant, sharp like that of an eagle so you can see far beyond the present. Samson was charmed by Delilah and because he didn't want to lose her, he told her the source of his great strength. Samson was fast asleep on Delilah's lap where he found comfort and was unaware that his hair had been shaved off. It's impossible to cut the hair of a lion unless it's been tamed by something which entices it. In our place of comfort, we tend to ignore most of the things or signs around us because we feel it's a place of safety. We need to be alert both in the storm and when at peace. Most people become spiritually active when they are trusting God for a miracle but once they have answers to their prayers, they become lukewarm and spiritually relaxed. They forget that the devil that tried to delay their blessings is strategizing on how to steal their miracles. You need to be alert to guard the blessings and miracles God has given you so that they will last longer. After Samson's hair had been shaved, he woke up and thought he would go against the Philistines and shake himself free, little did he know that the Lord had left him. Just like Samson, what are you charmed by? Have you entangled yourself with people like Delilah whose aim is to steal, kill, and destroy or the things of this world have blindfolded you? You may wake up and realize that your strength is gone. Be vigilant!

1 Corinthians 16:13

Be on your guard; stand firm in the faith; be courageous; be strong.

Sluggard syndrome

The result of laziness and sluggishness is unfruitfulness which could lead to poverty either physically or spiritually. A lazy man who leaves his farmland without pruning and maintenance will have his field full of weeds with little or no harvest. There are many lazy Christians who are inactive when it comes to working for the Master. They give all the available excuses to avoid doing the right thing because of their sluggishness. This brings us to the parable of the talents in the Bible. The master apportioned talents to his servants, each according to his ability; to one he gave five talents, to another he gave two while he gave the third servant one talent. The servants with the five and two talents invested their talents while the servant with one talent buried his talent, awaiting the return of his master. One would expect the servant who had one talent to put in all his resources and energy to make sure he maximizes that talent but he was rather sluggish with it. A lazy servant does not reap fruits nor does a lazy Christian. God expects us to bear fruits because Jesus is the true vine who supplies all the necessary nutrients needed for us to be fruitful. What happens to the branch that does not produce fruits? God does not waste His resources nor will He give us more assets than the capacity He has given us. We all need to be proactive and quit sluggishness with the work of the Master. Let us wake up from our sleep and be active in the service of the Master which is our loyalty to Him.

Proverbs 24:30 -34

I went past the field of a sluggard, past the vineyard of someone who has no sense; thorns had come up everywhere, the ground was covered with weeds, and the stone wall was in ruins. I applied my heart to what I observed and learned a lesson from what I saw: A little sleep, a little slumber, a little folding of the hands to rest— and poverty will come on you like a thief and scarcity like an armed man.

Careless Syndrome

Today, many people do not care for their souls, they live carelessly not minding what the repercussions would be. They ignore all the notable signals and fall deeply asleep amid danger. There is a great need to be more discerning about our lives and to be more disciplined in our decisions and actions. Many had slipped into spiritual poverty as a result of carelessness. In the body of Christ, many souls are spiritually negligent, and these are not visible from their physical appearance but one could easily discern this spiritually. It is, therefore, important and necessary for those who are spiritually alert to ensure that the unconscious souls are revived because we all are saved to rise for the salvation of others.

CHAPTER 8

Yield

There are lots of road signs warning us of what lies ahead and things we need to do while on the road. Some of the road signs include bumps ahead, animal crossing, speed limit, do not enter sign, traffic light, and so on. These signs are meant to guide us and they are not optional but mandatory for every driver to follow for safety. There are varieties of signs in our life's journey which must be obeyed in order to sail safely. These signs, if ignored, could be fatal. One of the advantages of obeying these signs is to reduce the stopping distance and force of impact in case there is a collision. How then do we know what lies ahead on the path we have never been to? The truth is, when we obey the instructions of those who have successfully trod the path, our safety is guaranteed. It's of paramount importance for us to be sensitive to the leading of the Holy Spirit as our guide. How do we know how He speaks to us when we don't know the identity of the person speaking? This brings us to spiritual sensitivity.

Spiritual sensitivity refers to the strength of spiritual reaction or response to one's spirit. This is about God inspiring His children to do His will through the power of the Holy Spirit. Oftentimes we ask the question, how does God speak to us? There are different ways through which He instructs us; speaking, vision/ dreams, a conviction in one's spirit, and sometimes through people, e.t.c. Growing up, I have asked numerous questions on how God speaks to His children. I was told that God speaks in diverse ways but the common way is through His Word or the Bible. I knew He spoke through His Word but believing that the Word written years before my existence applies to me seems unbelievable and unrealistic, so I reached a conclusion. If the Bible was written many years ago, how does it apply to me? Moreover, my name was not mentioned nor do I have the personality of the recipient. Trying to figure it out in my own wisdom made me put God in a box which is a ridiculous thing to do but as a child, that was the capacity my brain could fathom. Over time, with the intervention of the Holy Spirit, God began to unveil the mysteries and treasures in His Word and I strongly believed that if it is in the Bible, then it is mine through faith. I am from the Abrahamic generation and also a joint-heir with Christ in God's kingdom.

When God started to unravel the mysteries in His Word, the quest to hear from Him began. Studying and living the Word of God keeps us rooted in Christ so that when the flood and storms of life come, the nutrients derived from the Word of God will sustain us and give us victory. When you take time to meditate on God's Word with the help of God's Spirit, you receive an established revelation and truth about God's instructions guided by His will. The revelation of the Word of God is beyond the letters but the inspiration and impartation that comes from the Holy Spirit who is the greatest author. Being spoon-fed by people makes you believe solely in the preacher's messages whether they are true or false. However, digging deep into the Word of God confirms the preacher's message and gives us a personal revelation and light into the Word. The Bible gives an illustration about the Berean Jews who searched the scriptures to examine the validity of Paul and Silas' messages. Feeding your Spirit man with God's Word energizes and empowers you spiritually. It is the work of the Holy Spirit to sensitize and quicken your heart to be obedient to God in Spirit and in truth. One of the gifts of the Holy Spirit which God has given His children is a discerning spirit that enables you to determine the source of a motivation if it's from God, devil, or human reasoning.

Although God has diverse ways of communicating to His children, so does the devil. Knowing and understanding how God speaks to you is important. In the Bible, God spoke through dreams, prophets, and visions. We have perfect examples of people in the Bible that were sensitive to the leading of God's Spirit:

- God gave an assurance to Abraham through vision in Genesis 15:1.

- God gave a warning to Abimelech against taking Sarah in his dreams in Genesis 20.

- God gave inheritance of Bethel to Jacob through a dream in Genesis 28.

- God called Samuel into ministry through a vision in 1 Samuel 3.

- God gave Solomon an open offer in his dream in 1 Kings 3:5.

- God gave Daniel messages about the nation of Israel and the future in his dream in Daniel 2.

- God spoke to Joseph in his dream to seek refuge in Egypt with Mary and Jesus Matthew 2:13.

- God spoke to Cornelius through a vision that led to the salvation of his household in Acts 10.

- God confirmed the vision given to Cornelius by speaking to Peter in a vision in Acts 10.

- God spoke to John through visions while he was on the Island of Patmos which resulted in the book of Revelation.

From the aforementioned examples in the Bible, it is obvious how God dealt with these people and many others. How He ordered their steps into perfection and guidance answers the question "How do we distinguish between God's instructions, human reasoning, and the devil's manipulations?" The devil, on the other hand, brings in fear, doubts, and torment into the hearts of people. Oftentimes, people make the mistake of accepting every inspiration or word they receive as the Word of God. Remember that the devil tempted Jesus three times and you are not an exception. There is no word spoken to you from God that does not have a foundation or validation in the Bible. This confirms that the Bible should be the standard and mirror of our lives. The Bible says test the spirits in 1 John 4:1. The ideal concept to distinguish between the voice of God and devil is to pray and study the Word which enables you to recognise the spirit of truth and the spirit of falsehood.

God's Word came to many Biblical characters as warnings and signs concerning what was to come and what steps they should take to ensure their safety. Imagine what would have happened if they were spiritually insensitive to God's instructions. They would have ended up in perdition. It is a necessity to walk with God's leading in this journey, obeying all His instructions and ignoring none. Why do we need the GPS to navigate? Mostly because it helps to achieve greater efficiency, but the Holy Spirit has revolutionized our daily lives much more than the physical GPS because GPS is limited to a physical zone which cannot navigate the spiritual things. Most times, when we ignore the GPS and decide to follow our paths, we end up on a longer route or in an unsafe zone. In order to navigate through life's journey easily and in safety, the Holy Spirit is one person we cannot afford to walk without. He makes life easier for you and just the way you would drive confidently in a new environment with the help of the GPS, you can walk through life with great confidence that you have the greatest guide on board with you.

Conclusion

You need to yield the right of way to the Holy Spirit if you want to navigate through life successfully. Just as it is mandatory to have a valid driver's license which gives you eligibility to be on the road, so do you need the Holy Spirit on your journey. The Holy Spirit is one companion you can never do without because He serves as your instructor, guide, teacher, and confidant. As the forerunner who has gone the way ahead of you, He knows what lies ahead and what dangers you need to keep away from. Who is a forerunner? According to the dictionary, "A forerunner is a person or thing that precedes the coming or development of someone or something else" In this case, Jesus is our forerunner who had trod the path which we are treading. Need I say that the anointing of the Holy Spirit made Jesus' journey a successful one and not just because He was the Son of God?

Hebrews 6:19-20

"This hope we have as an anchor of the soul, both sure and steadfast, and which enters the Presence behind the veil, where the forerunner has entered for us, even Jesus, having become High Priest forever according to the order of Melchizedek."

We follow the Holy Spirit because He has gone ahead of us and because He is leading us to a place of safety. Nobody makes a failed man his mentor, everyone wants to follow a successful man, most importantly one who has carved a successful pathway for others to follow. The disciples followed Jesus because they trusted Him to take them to safety being the way, the truth, and the life. After Jesus' death, they had to wait for the impartation of the Holy Spirit as commanded by Jesus because without the Holy Spirit, they could do nothing. On the day of Pentecost, when the disciples were baptised with the Holy Spirit and fire, they had a great encounter with powerful evidence which enabled them to do greater works. The importance of the Holy Spirit in our Christian journey cannot be overemphasized. There is a need to move from the ankle level anointing to being fully immersed in the Holy Spirit because it is impossible to live a successful Christian life without Him. The Holy spirit enables us to walk in the full dimension of God's power. These dimensions as described by Ezekiel are ankle level, knee level, loin level, and full immersion.

Ezekiel 47:1-5

Afterward he brought me again unto the door of the house; and, behold, waters issued out from under the threshold of the house eastward: for the forefront of the house stood toward the east, and the waters came down from under from the right side of the house, at the south side of the altar. Then brought him out of the way of the gate north ward, and led me about the way without unto the utter gate by the way that looketh eastward; and, behold, there ran out waters on the right side. And when the man that had the line in his hand went forth eastward, he measured a thousand cubits, and he brought me through the waters; the waters were to the ankles. Again he measured a thousand, and brought me through the waters; the waters were to the knees. Again he measured a thousand, and brought me through; the waters were to the loins. Afterward he measured a thousand; and it was a river that I could not pass over: for the waters were risen, waters to swim in, a river that could not be passed over.

The ankle, knee, and loin levels - At these degrees, we find ourselves struggling between our flesh and the Holy Spirit. This was Paul's experience in Romans 7:19, 21 -23. His desire was to do good but he kept doing the evil he did not desire to do. We tend to lean on religion when we operate on any of these degrees, however, the Holy Spirit stirs us up for spiritual depth which is beyond religion's shallowness when we operate in a higher dimension which is total absorption.

Full immersion indicates the fullness of His anointing. At this measure, we are no longer controlled by the flesh but in total submission to the will of the Holy Spirit. This water cannot be passed over because of its depth, an indication that the Holy Spirit is fully in charge and there is no pathway for the flesh to operate.

Revelation 22:1

And he shewed me a pure river of water of life, clear as crystal, proceeding out of the throne of God and of the Lamb.

This water flows to us through the Holy Spirit for the fullness of God. This is the measure we should desire and aspire to attain in our Christian journey so that our lives will be less of us but more of God with the aim of overflowing to the world around us. Conclusively, the Holy spirit makes all these spiritual and kingdom principles achievable with no complications and fatality.

www.ingramcontent.com/pod-product-compliance
Lightning Source LLC
LaVergne TN
LVHW010119170826
845678LV00012B/2496

* 9 7 8 1 7 3 8 7 5 4 6 3 2 *